# MY BODY
## BOOK FOR TODDLERS

# THIS BOOK BELONGS TO

..........................................................

Toddlers are fascinated by their eyes,
ears, nose, fingers and toes.

This book is a great way to introduce little ones
to the vocabulary of body parts and have big fun
while doing it!

trace your hand
with Mom and Dad

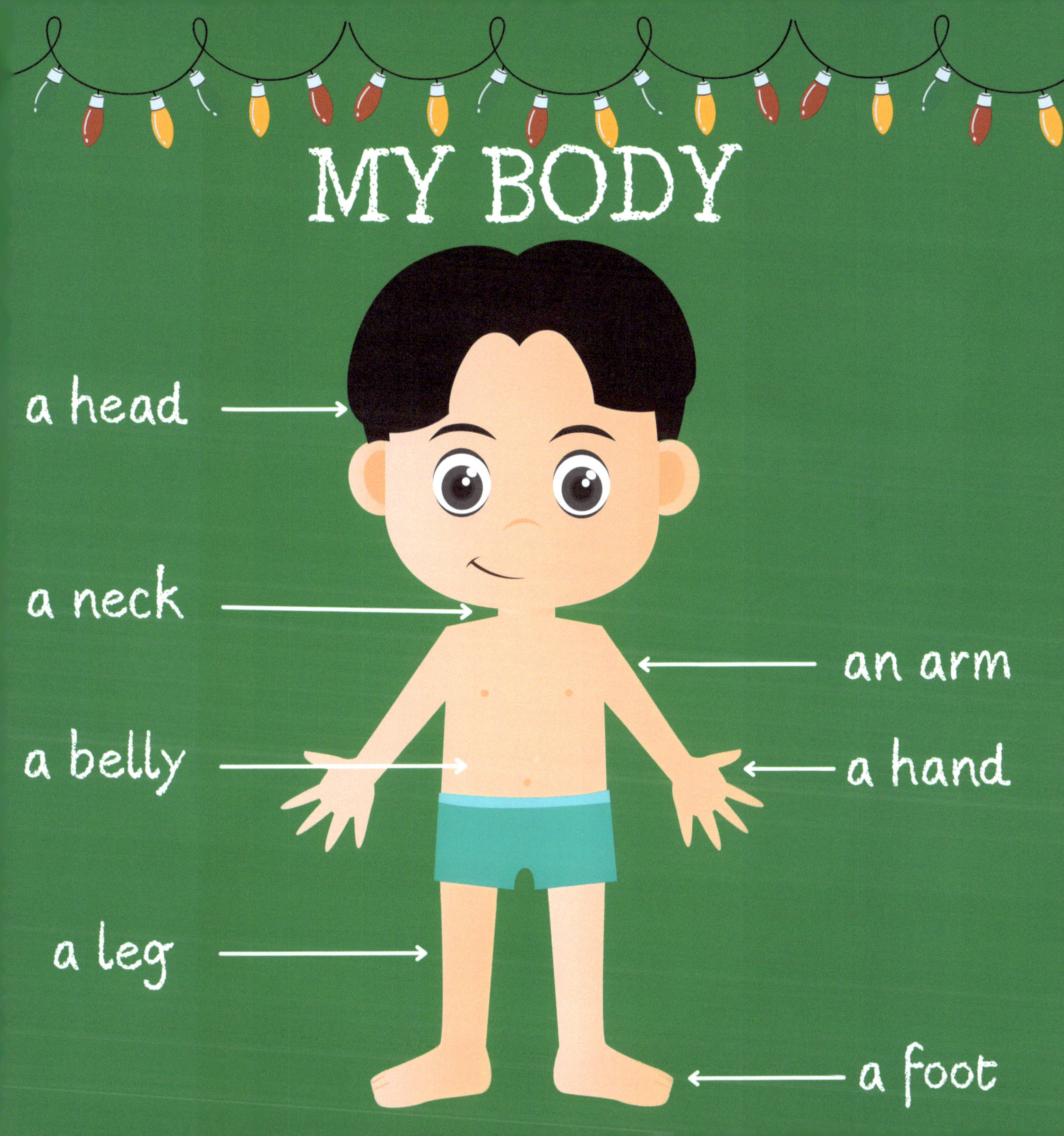# MY BODY

trace your foot
with Mom and Dad

# MY HANDS and FEET

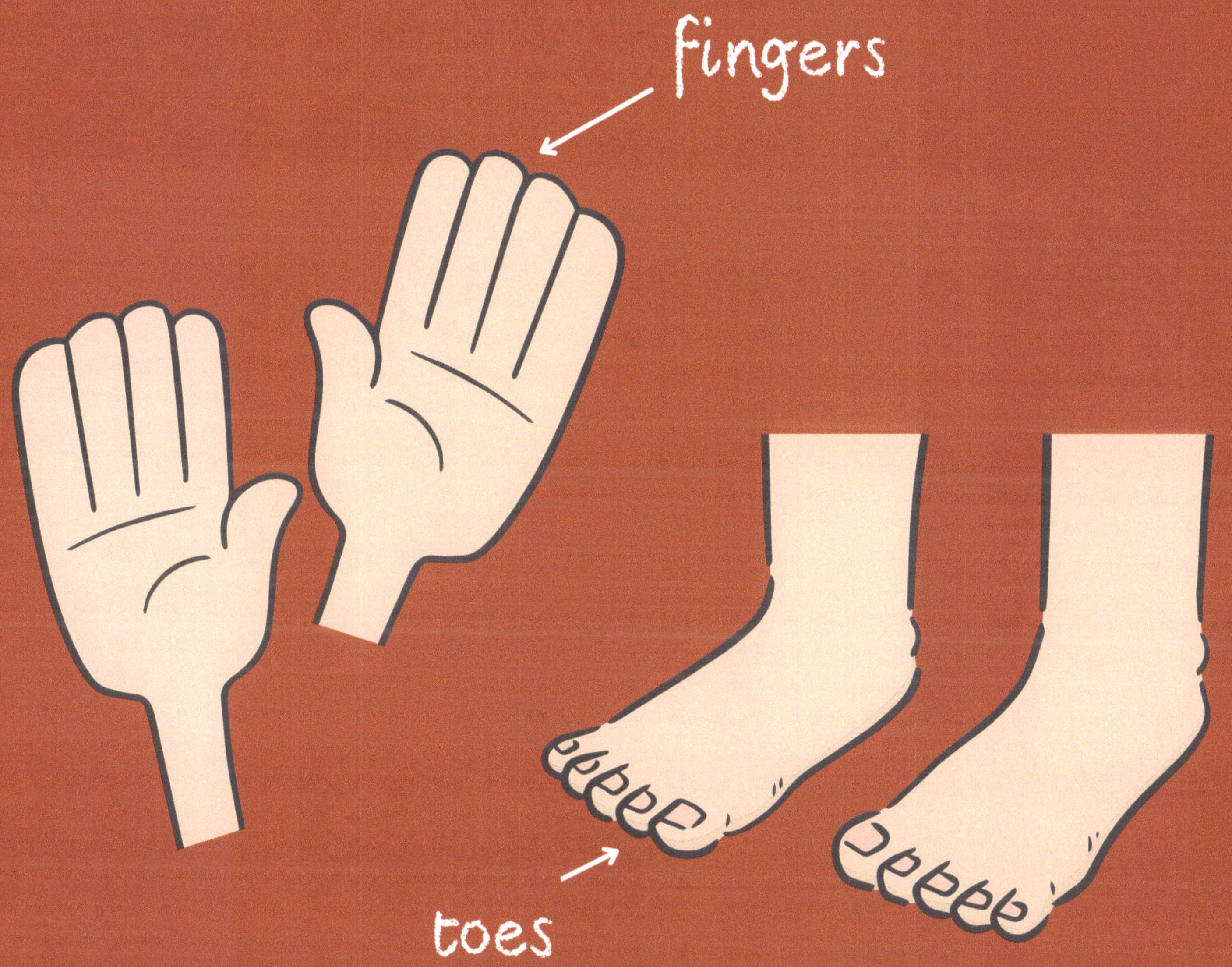

give the kiss
to Mom and Dad

# MY FACE

point the eye
of Mom and Dad

# MY EYES

People may have eyes
of different colours!

brown eyes

blue eyes

green eyes

smell the flower
with Mom and Dad

MY NOSE

stick out your tongue
with Mom and Dad

# MY MOUTH

whisper in the ear
of Mom and Dad

# MY EARS

lough out loud
with Mom and Dad

# CAN YOU REPEAT THIS SOUND?

cry out loud
with Mom and Dad

# CAN YOU REPEAT THIS SOUND?

clap your hands
with Mom and Dad

# CAN YOU REPEAT THIS SOUND?

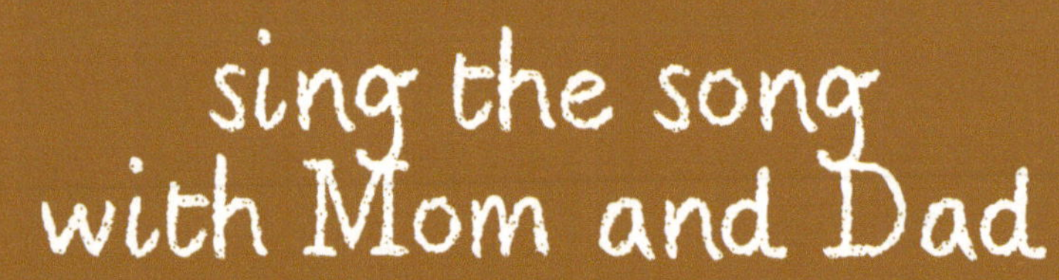

sing the song
with Mom and Dad

# CAN YOU REPEAT THIS SOUND?

Merry
Christmas